JERSEY SHORTS

Writing for My Life: A Collection of Poems and Stories

LEANNE COSENTINO

NEWMAN SPRINGS PUBLISHING
320 Broad Street
Red Bank, NJ 07701

First originally published by Newman Springs Publishing 2024

ISBN 979-8-89308-466-5 (Paperback)
ISBN 979-8-89308-468-9 (Digital)

Printed in the United States of America

CONTENTS

INTRODUCTION
Returning from the Tide

It has been years since I could hear the word *cancer* without cringing…the memory of the smell of sterility from the hospital, the recognizable look of deathlike paleness on the patients' faces, my husband's falling asleep inevitably during the never-ending waiting for doctors and their tests and checkups, chemotherapy and radiation treatments. Life goes on, regardless of past sufferings and people say goodbye all the time yet survive and with hope and faith manage to be happy again with time.

It was during my cancer *staycation* that I took the time to smell and write about the roses, to reconsider my collection of poems and short stories and organize my life through the memories recorded in my computer and in many journals. The collection is meant to guide readers through tough times, whether personally or worldly and to reiterate the beliefs held by many who continue to "put their best foot forward" in the face of adversity and loss.

The collection is dedicated to my precious mother Victoria Barbagli Clark, my joy, best friend, and the inspiration for all my writing over the years. The book I promised has finally emerged, as raw and full of hard truths and edits as was necessary for its completion. I know you wanted me to be known for something helpful and special and encouraged me to do things you never had the courage to do yourself, so this one is for you, Mom!

All my love forever and a sunny day,

Your Lee

1
Being Strong and Moving Along (Beach "Shorts")

What's in a Name?

A secret understanding
we share on the beach…
You sit a block away in solitary silence—
the ocean waves whispering
your hidden name to me.
Friends are near, but I am all yours—
lost in the misty breeze brushing
your soft lips over my body

A secret understanding
we share on the beach—
Silent, subtle…steady as the tide…
My heart beating, wildly,
In rhythm with the earth's soul

Wednesday: First Date

Thanks for the dinner,
And I loved the dessert.
But that look on your face—
Honey, that hurt!
That look on your face,
I can't bear to see,
For I know it so well—
It's a curse on me.
You can make me only as happy as I can be!

Trials

Your disapproval has branded me
Like a searing hot iron.
Everywhere I look
My body blisters with the pain.

In some places
Scars will remain.

True Love

You are
    an exotic
    butterfly   and

        my net
         has a giant

           HOLE

Single Socks

Socks are the sluts of the laundry world—
Can be found always sneaking around
Hiding out on their own—
Whereabouts of their partner unknown—
Single socks desperately cling to most anything!

Sunday

You made me so happy
Taking me to see the blues.
Then you made me so blue
Trying to make me happy!

Dirty Little Poem

I'd like to be an ice cube
floating in your drink,
pressing firmly
against your soft lips,
your warm tongue,
hitting me by chance,
would make me melt

The Kiss?

Far better than the real one
Is the kiss denied.
It lasts for days and days
Playing through my mind.

Spring Cling

Bad news surrounds me.
Death by accident,
good health starved by disease.
Of survival in this world,
little guarantees,
For disaster and grief
lurk under cover of safeties.

Outside, the world offers little certainty,
Snow clings to spring cherry blossoms
And reminds me why I am drawn to your stability—
By closing off all else, you bring the world to me!

Love in Bloom

Red roses bloom
in the vase
in my room
and also
in the garden
of my heart.
I love you.

The Christmas Gifts

I wish gifts for you
as vast as the sea
As bright as the moon—
But can give you
only my dreams
of beautiful moments

forming an eternity
between us—
your whispers of love
creating a picture of light
shining down
onto what was once
only a garden of shadow.

Hope Is a Dangerous Thing

You presented me
To a stranger
When I introduced you
To my heart:

My spirit waiting,
Opened
Your heart remaining,
Closed

Under lockdown,
Your emotions
Bound by fear,
Your feelings
Masked by insecurity:

My spirit,
Broken,
Trying to
Free yours.

The Rescue

Let me open you up—
Show you to your
Inner light—
Help you to see
All that could be.

Who will do
The same for me—
When you relock the door
And throw away my key?

32 and Blue

The flowers
you bought
for my birthday
died
before they
had a chance
to fully bloom.

Dear Prince-Not-So-Charming

i   am   sorry
i   could   not   be
the   robot   girlfriend
whom   you   seek.

better luck   with the new model   next   week

As the Tides Roll Away

Dude, when I saw on my porch
The beach chair *like*
Previously entrusted to your care,
Bro, I knew, *for sure*,
Though safely out of harm's way,
The sun had *finally* set on our *awesome* beach day!

Toothbrushes

I threw out your toothbrush today.

I don't know why
It was so important for me
To preserve it so carefully for so long
Hidden in the bottom drawer
Of the bathroom cabinet.

Maybe it was because I still laugh out loud
Remembering when you told me your dream
Of being chased by giant toothbrushes
The night after I bought it for you.

I don't know why
It was so important for me
To throw it out today—
Lying "belly up" with my broken heart
In the bottom layer
Of the bathroom wastebasket

The Rock and the Wave

Days after you told me
That after all these years together
There was nothing further to discuss about us,
I walked out on to the jetty
Where once we had time for small talk.

As I observed the swirling water
Constantly washing over rocks,
It reminded me of us.
Waves wash over rocks, changing them
To some degree—
Molding them,
Shaping them,
Caressing them.
But they remain rocks in the end.

Though dripping wet with your aura,
Your influence,
Your love,
Your rejection,
I'll be moving up on the igneous scale—
To quartz, topaz, even diamond!
No more Talc-like behavior for me—
When I dry off in the sun sparklingly free!

A New Kind of Blind Date

He wants me to bring "my writing"…
Doesn't have any clue
That it's something I wear about my person
Rather than confine to one object.

Besides, I'm not putting all my words
Into anyone else's book anymore anyway.
Certain circumstances—
stolen journal, broken heart—
prevent me from keeping my feelings
all in one place.

As for this "meeting of the minds,"
Expectations—I have few;
Assumptions—I make none.

For the excitement lies
In the possible—
Not in the probable!

2

Rich or Poor
Down and Out at the Jersey Shore

Numbers Tell a Story

The way I estimate,
1/2 my life has been spent
searching for someone like you.

If it doesn't work out,
I realize I might have to spend
the other 1/2 missing your love.

25 taken from 35 leaves
10 years in remainder;
35 over 25 just doesn't make sense.

No matter how I do the math,
I can't find a common enough denominator
Between our numbers…

Yet the 2 of us have become 1.

You know,
I never cared much for math anyway!

Dating Ten Years Apart

It was an easy step…
Taken with full awareness.

If it was a step
Back
Or even a step

      Down

So be it.

It was an easy step…

      But…

I envision myself moving forward
To walk beside you on the path of life.

Instead I walk in a circle
Of a maze ten layers thick.

Around and around I go
Trying to catch up to you
Catching up to me.

The C. R. Game

We are playing a game
Called The Casual Relationship
We suspend all rules for this game—
Set up "safety guidelines" instead

To be eligible for the C. R. Game
You need to be confused and indecisive
It helps to be insecure as well—
That way your opponent will be well-matched

The object of the game is to escape unscathed
We make our moves carefully
Trying to keep our feelings in check
Waiting to see who will hurt or be hurt first

Eventually, the C. R. Game will end
Someone will be less than careful
Or one of us will quit the other
In a game without rules, no one can win

Decoy

While walking around the inlet
One clear but cold day,
I noticed a decoy of an owl—
So carefully planted
On the upper railing of a deck.
And I thought about you
With much affection,
But not with much more certainty
Than a circling owl
Looking for life's partner
And finding only wood.

Not so discerning as the wise owl,
I fall for the woodwork instead,
Circling around small, insignificant details of our meetings—
The way the cat placed his woobie between your shoes—
Marking you as his territory, and so soon, like his owner.

We laughed at his complaints in the morning—
Bonded when you said he was asking his mommy for food.

Why do I concentrate on those endearing details—
Like how you so carefully put away the iron
And made the bed on your first stay-over—
And not on the fact that you forget the days I work late—
Or that you asked me twenty times (at least)
If I'd seen the same movie?
Yes, I do know that we are both your current favorites!

Spider and Fly

Seeing beyond you, I love what could be—
You spin a web of dreams around me.
Instead of walking by your side,
I follow blindly, close behind
Dizzy in a cloud ten sticky fibers wide.
I love more than just what my eyes see—
You spin a web of dreams around me.
Too late before I realize
You're crawling behind, instead,
You've fallen out of reach
And trapped us both inside your web!

I Love You, But...

When you tell me you love me—
Why does it sound like "the end"?
Or a prolonged goodbye?
Why do you say it at all
If you know it's said with regret?
You ought to just come right out
And say, "I regret that I love you."

True love comes with smiles
And open hearts—
Not fear and regrets.

Love me—
Doubt free-
Or let me be!

At What Cost?

Though I offer my love to you freely,
You are cautious to accept it as such
Could it be that you're afraid—
Or maybe you know too much?

Grief has taught you
That nothing in life worthwhile
Comes without a price or false smile

You falter on accepting my generous offer
You think somewhere—
I've hidden the coffer

If you accept my gift,
What would be the sacrifice?
Will it be sugar and spice
And everything nice?

Or loss of some freedom
You've taken for granted?
You'll never know
Until you've accepted

What if you put me off for so long
That I rescind?
At what cost
To have me lost?

A Marriage Masterpiece

A good marriage is a work of art,
The partners are painters,
Bringing their visions to the blank canvas,
Creating a masterpiece one stroke at a time.

Some strokes are heavy and dark,
Casting dull shadows on the canvas.
Others are effortless and bright,
Adding balance and grace to the picture.

Whether the paint be thick or thin—
More or less colorful than imagined—
Determined artists have a knack
For glossing over minor mistakes.

As time treads over the canvas,
Different hues may be added
Delineating triumphs and failures
And blending separate details into one.

After years shared together,
The artists' visions gradually morph
Revealing their unique love expression—
A priceless marriage masterpiece!

Rheumatoid Arthritis Diagnosis

I always liked *The Wizard of Oz*
But oddly enough, this disease
Reminds me of the Tin Man;
The stiffness now defines me.

Every morning is like a rain shower
For these joints—heavy as rusted metal—
My doctors' trial-and-error remedies
Not nearly as effective as Dorothy's and Scarecrow's.

I attempt to move my hands
Through the tingling numbness;
The excruciating pain in my fingers
Makes it impossible to clutch a wooden ax.

Instead, I swing out of bed—
Elbows and knees bent
And tight as golf clubs,
Feet huge and frozen—
Clunk-clunking around
In need of giant silver shoes.

Last night, again, I dreamed of gymnastics—
My body flowing effortlessly over parallel bars;
Wrists and ankles wrapped, but strong,
Supporting my muscles during acrobatics.

My mind does the cartwheels now—
Trying to make sense of this sudden, daily mystery
And wondering why the diets, the supplements,
The medications are not working.

Silver paint and wooden ax aside,
I am feeling like the Tin Man.
Except…
At least, he had his oil can.

Fifteen Months to Just Us

Mortified,
Sentenced—not tried,
I left you at the courthouse
To begin your hard time.

Bound to your crime
And bound to me—
Your sentence seems an eternity.
Your hands in cuffs, and mine set free,
Soon "just-us" became "just-me"!

"Justice, said Ms. Judgment,
would have to be served."
But justice is a funny word.

The words she used to seal your fate:
"Reprehensible, unforgivable," and wait—
"Your past was troublesome, and
are you chewing gum?"

The cough drop came from me to you
to calm your nerves, but not to chew!
Justice, "just-us," I thought,
As against the laughter and tears I fought.

Then Her Honor handed down the time—
The sentence didn't fit the crime.
Whose punishment? Yours and mine!

Ms. Judgment tried to call for more
As the bailiff led you near the door,
And when they shackled you to the bench—
My heart began to sink and wrench.

Until you blew me a kiss goodbye—
You met my gaze eye-to-eye,
"Remember, do not let them see you cry."

Then hope arose inside my heart—
For I knew not even "mis-justice"
Would tear our love apart!

Ice Storm on V-Day

Ice storm—
Trees frozen in crystal ice,
Shining in the warm sun,
But not melting.

Tears form freezing daggers
On my warm eyelashes,
As I cry outside in the cold
Without you by my side
To share life's wonders and joys.

Yet we share this sorrow—
Two hearts, frozen together
With the knowledge
That nothing else,

Not even life's wondrous mysteries,
Can mean a thing
Without our love to warm us.

We are two crystal trees,
Glowing defiantly bright
In the winter's sun,
Blinded by love—
Frozen, solidly, in time…

First Day of Spring

Looking out over the fading day
Horizon gray with black clouds
Night is on its way
Grass frozen in spots
Sprouting in others

I glimpse the sun setting through the clouds
Trying to make its last hurrah of the day
Trying to stay
Pushing those clouds back to winter
Where they belong
Stay in winter
Let our spring begin
We need to hope again
That maybe this is all behind us

Our winter is leaving
Hurray, hurray
I see the sun
Trying to come back
Like you are
Fighting your way through the clouds,
The darkness, the gray areas

Blocking the harshness, the humiliation,
The sadness you've had to face
While held captive in eternal winter
Spring waits for winter like I wait for you
Because my love is true
Pushing aside the clouds of doubt
I see the white inside the gray
And throw the black away
For spring begins this day!

Virtual Sex, True Love

Mental sex will have to do,
for now, for me, and for you.

Wish it were real,
my strength returning like steel.

Missing you terribly, patiently, daily,
loving you more and more intensely.

Wishing you a happy birthday,
knowing you'll return any day.

With my hope your keeper,
Our love grows deeper.

I will be deep in your arms, hopefully,
With you deeply in love inside me.

Independence Day for Some

I've been listening to the rain pouring down
Wishing in it this lonely feeling would drown.
When are you coming home free?
How many more months without me?

My baby's stuck at South Woods
It's been seven months since I've had all his goods
When's he coming home, you say?
He'll be on that list any stinking day!

Fireworks crackling all through the night
But not like the ones we make just right.
Brightly blazing colors in the sky
Can't compare with the sparkle in your eye,
Nor the touch of your hand on my thigh.

My baby's stuck at South Woods
It's been seven months since I've had all his goods
When's he coming home, you ask?
It's up to the state to fulfill that task!

Independence Day has a new meaning for us
Forget about the barbecues and all that fuss
Remember you're free now to enjoy the wealth
That comes from believing in oneself!

My baby's stuck at South Woods
It's been seven months since I've had all his goods
His heart's as peaceful as a dove
Now he's learned the true power of love!

Talbot Hall Blues

If you are minimum security
Serving hard time in New Jersey
You may be rehabilitated in Kearny
Behind the wall at Talbot Hall

At Talbot Hall, they've put up a wall
Of stipulations and regulations
To test your level of frustration
In the name of inmate "education"

Under the guise of Justice for All
And to make the residents feel small
They use demerits and affirmations
To assess the inmates' aggravations

In the place called Talbot Hall
They've designed a protective wall
So the Department of Corrections
Can use rules instead of weapons

Six pairs of sox and pants allowed
Wear your own T-shirts looking proud
Those with no help from family
Stand out sadly in the crowd

Play no cards or dice and place no bets
But ten full packs of cigarettes
May be delivered weekly through the mail
One more pack could send you back to jail

Waiting in line to bring your stuff
I can't stop thinking enough is enough
I stare at the herd of smoking men
Trying not to think about the time again

Weekends I wait in line just to see your smile
And to kiss you hello for a very short while
We eat your favorite food to lighten the mood
And say goodbye always too soon

Riding home so far in the peace of my car
I know love is much stronger than any wall
And my man's a wild-spirited horse
Thirsting to break through life's stall

With the help of programmed intervention
And plenty of deep introspection
That wall seems rather small
For a man who's ready to climb, not crawl

With six pairs of underwear and a heart full of care
My baby's learned that his feelings were meant to share
Thanks to the law at the place called Talbot Hall
My man's stepping out from behind his self-made wall

Time to move on from therapeutic instruction
And await Parole's approval or rejection
Please don't delay, send him home halfway
Because behind the Talbot Hall Wall my baby can't stay

Release him to me so I can play my part
After all my man is half my heart
My baby is a piece of work indeed
And I'm a workaholic in dire need!

So if you ever reside at Talbot Hall
Remember to stand up proud and tall
Don't be afraid to open a door in your wall
Make it justice for one and for all!

There's a Stranger in My House

There's a stranger in my house—
His name is Mr. Addiction
Just when things are getting good—
He strolls into my life unexpectedly
Changing my plans so selfishly—
And hanging around indefinitely

I am always surprised to see Mr. A.
For he nonchalantly edges into my life
As gloomily as clouds before a storm—
Sputtering rain on my beach day,
Dampening fun-loving explorations
And peaceful nature expeditions

Don't forget about family events—
Mr. Addiction loves those best—
Surprises are his favorite, you know,
But holidays are even worse
Mr. addiction will be sure to show up
Even in someone else's house
To "de-gift" me from any holiday cheer

What became of the plan?
And where is my man?
He's been replaced again
By the imposter in my house,
A stranger called Mr. Addiction

Though you think I'd be forewarned
Somehow Mr. Addiction sneaks by me
At times, almost undetectably—
I'm blinded by hope that he'll be thwarted
By the sheer strength of your love for me

Just as my hope begins to win out
I realize I've been duped again
By this trickster in my house,
A stranger called Mr. Addiction

His specialty is manipulation
But he's not above intimidation
Or just plain and simple lying
For Mr. Addiction stares me down
As if I am to blame for being surprised, stupefied,
Or downright disgusted by his behavior

Who is to blame, then, for this mistake?
It's Mr. Addiction who always takes the cake
Although I have let him stay,
He's been an unwanted guest to this day

It's all Mr. Addiction's fault, you see?
But you're letting him get the best of you and me
Again, I've been outsmarted
By the stranger in my house,
The stranger called Mr. Addiction

If you are unable to decipher
A message from this writing
Look deep inside to find the stranger lurking
When you finally catch him,
Tell him I just want my husband
I'm done with this game of hiding-and-seeking

But, alas, you will never be free
Unless you show him the way out
Because we've both been outsmarted
By the stranger in our house,
The stranger called Mr. Addiction

Our Second Chance

Some things are better left unsaid
But not this
I love you
I love you should always be said

Some things are better left alone
But not me
I've missed you
I'm not completely me without you

People wonder if I've been lonely
They couldn't possibly know
I've never been less
Since you've begun to grow

You're coming home soon
A strange kind of excitement
Brews in me—our future beginning
A chance to renew our start in life

Remember that most people
Don't get two seconds—
Chances that is—
One is the true-love limit

Time to grab for the stars,
The moon, our dreams
Let's have no more excuses
For brand-new life within our reach

I love you
Says more than most people
Express to each other
In a whole lifetime

Some things are better left unsaid
But not I love you
It's not so easy to say
Yet all I need to believe

3

Lost and Found Cancer Files

Jane: A Lost and Found Poem
(For my beloved grandmother who changed
her name but not her fate)

She tells me her story
Repeats it over and over again
And on this special day
I'm finally ready to listen

Her parents' dream to own a farm
For her, it was a nightmare
The heat, the bugs, the snakes that jump
Always would give her a scare

Picking vegetables outside in the sun
Inside the dust of dirt floors
No friends in isolation
Just farming and doing other chores

At sixteen, she runs away to get married
Seeing hope for a better life
Finding out all too soon
There's no escape in being a wife

Offers me words of wisdom
Experienced from her own life
With regret, talks of days long gone
Lessons about struggle and strife

Releases a flood of memories
Which I soak up most carefully
For I know her pain—her history—
Lives and dies in me

Too soon now she's gone from this world
Leaving behind our family legacy
Although I've lost my grandmother
I've found more of her inside me

(July 15, 2001)

Christmas 2000

Christmas time may come and go
But a mother's love will constantly grow
I know that she loves me, no matter what the strife—
Thanks for the gifts—the looks, your love, my life!

Connie
(For my stepmother-in-law, who faced colon cancer with
unbelievable dignity, grace, and style; and for my father-
in-law who suffered the loss of two wives to cancer)

C is for Connie-Mom
That's who you'll always be to me
C is for Constance—as in Constant—
Like your love for friends and family

C for Classy—the perfect word for you
Your elegance spanned from head-to-shoe
C for Chic—always buying gifts in a stylish boutique
A Cosmopolitan lover of the unique antique

C for Clinician—freely offering friendly motherly advice
Your kind words to lift my spirits were more than just nice
C for Counselor—when things just weren't right
You were in my corner through many a dark night

C for Courageous—leaving many of us in complete awe
Of our brave mom, wife, sister, nona, and mother-in-law
For the way you faced your battle was a sight to befall
Your faith and gentle grace left a life-long impression on us all

C for Concetta—your nickname in certain company
Exuding a shabby-chic taste—with a twist of French Country
How you loved traveling to Martha's Vineyard, and especially Italy
C for Cosentino—your heart always and forever belongs to JC.

C for Caring—sharing lovely treasures from your holiday
Never forgetting a friend or loved one's birthday
C for Cherish—wish we'd had so much more time with you
Bonding family together while our admiration grew

C is for Composure—God's gift to us—your tranquil Closure
You left us with a peaceful and loving final adieu
Your love was our blessing—we all hope that you knew
And so, from now until forever, we love you!

(October 16, 2009)

Iago
(bright eyes, yellow and wide; owned each other
for seventeen years with love and pride)

"Iags"
My faithful and beloved pet
Suddenly
Suddenly you are gone

Though people will say
But you had seventeen years together
Together for seventeen years yet
So altogether
Suddenly gone

Suddenly you are gone
From my grasp
Missing from my lap
Your little basket bed left empty in the corner

How could it be?
You're now in my memory
So suddenly
After seventeen years?

Though it's day one of spring
A wicked wind blows through here
I shiver with a cold chill
And reach for your warmth
But suddenly
You are no longer mine—
Except in loss

I wander around the house
For a long time—
Like a lost child
And stop at your old haunts—
Suddenly
I realize you will never
Walk, sleep, hide, or groom
In these places ever again

Unable to control the volcanic
Eruption of tears and mucus
That has become my face
I break down and kneel by your food dish
To inspect your leftover dry food
As if it's the first time I've seen cat food—
I never noticed before that it had the cutest shapes…

The sight of the lunchmeat scraps,
Our last attempt to feed you,
Makes my heart beat with despair
Our favorite ritual, halted, suddenly

Suddenly I realized
I had kept my promise—
That when you stopped eating
I would know it was time

The decision was impossible
With those bright yellow eyes,
And shiny, smooth jet black fur
You were too beautiful for death

Though I knew the vet was coming,
I emptied and changed your water,
Scooped your litter box nice and clean
And made sure you didn't have poops
Stuck and crusted over in your eyes

Suddenly they were here to do it
You and I had run out of time
Suddenly
After seventeen years
All that's left is tears

So suddenly, just like that,
After taking your last cat nap on my lap
I can't bear that you're gone
Faithful pet of so long
Carried off like a beautiful sleeping doll

No longer my comforting sleeping partner
Cuddling like a spoon behind my knees
Waking me up just before the alarm
To sing me your favorite morning cat song

Suddenly
My baby has left me
And I don't know what to do
Will I never stop listening, looking, longing for you?

(With love always from your cat-mom, March 20, 2008)

How Much Time to Get Over Your Cat?
(A Poem in Progress)

A month later
I am still wondering…
How much time to get over your cat's passing?

It's time to get this poem written
For I know if I don't write it
The time will pass by too slowly
And I won't have made any progress
Toward getting over it anyway

Time can't steal away our memories
Be they good or bad, happy, or sad
But tricks us instead
Burdening us with our sorry worries
Clouding us with a lack of gratitude
Altering our values for the worse

By the time we've realized
What this scoundrel's been up to
It's too late to change our behaviors
And we are left behind to revel in our failures

We should be reveling in our good times
Not remembering what's passed with regret
Time doesn't care for our "what-ifs"
So neither should we.
It's not as though we could rewind
Our mistakes, missteps, misfortunes
And right what's wrong—
That time's come and gone

After all, what does it really matter?
We grieve for our precious pets
All the time playing Time's fools
So now, a year later,
I've decided no longer to wonder:
How much time to get over your cat?

Let's just live in the moment
Playful as kittens and carefree
Like puppy dogs and children

As long as time permits
Celebrate the life of a pet—
Short, happy, and full of good memories

(April 20, 2008–March 20, 2009)

Ode to Cicero
(for Pop with deepest sympathy, December 18, 2010)

You were a lot of attitudes
In a small, white puff of fluff
Around the yard, you were just skipping
And now I'm left here with you missing

Like a tiny ballerina-dancer
Front-legs out, you stood your ground—
Though you stunk just like a skunk
How I miss having you around…

Oh, Oh, Cicero—
Why'd you go and leave me—
Don't you know?
I'm feeling so, so alone…

Oh, Oh, Cicero—
At certain people, you snapped
And yapped alike for friend and foe
Now the quiet's left me feeling so low…

Oh, Oh, Cicero—
How could I know?
That you would go
And leave me so full of woe…

You barked the alphabet
I never knew how much it meant
Your sassiness I'll never forget
On missing you like this, I'd never have bet

Oh, Oh, Cicero—
Why'd you have to leave me so full of woe?
I'm so full of woe,
For my Cicero

The Knockout Roses
(A poem for my father)
November 2016

Knockout roses were developed to be hardy no doubt
they make it through cancer, depression, and drought
like you make it through every week, taking it on bought by bought
That's why the knockout roses remind me of you
They bloom throughout the seasons—in winter too

Because the knockout rose bush blooms throughout the year
I planted it below my bedroom window to fill my view with cheer
It's close to the house and even closer to my heart—
as reliable and persistent as my father is smart
It symbolizes cultivated beauty, everlasting love, and much more

as in the houses of Lancaster and York—red and white roses at war
But these roses are always peacefully in bloom underneath my bedroom

Knockout roses set the standard for adaptability, color, and size
their staggered thorns protect the petals both sweet and wise
Resisting disease, they look good in any landscape
and drop off leaves independently when they become out of shape
High in drama and vitamin C—
The roses signify the best of you in me
From early spring to final frost
my love of knockout roses is never lost
You might never know if you gave them a quick glance
because knockout roses don't make it just by chance!
They were born to be determined, diligent, and fair
and remind me that thanks to you I can look good without hair

My knockout roses were brought here by you
and continue to grow no matter what I can or cannot do
I love them so much because they never show their trump card
without complaint, they grow despite the rawness of the yard

These roses inherited your roots, and under my window, they thrive
Inside my cancer retreat, I watch them and know it's good to be alive
Because of knockout roses, I have hope from your example of the
will to survive

Centered under my window, your gift of knockout roses grow to my
surprise and delight
And remind me every day of how you have never given up the living-
well-with-cancer fight

My knockout roses shine with everlasting beautiful light
We will never forget our love of roses even after we have said good night

(Resting peacefully with the birds in the South Jersey woods, August
9, 2017)

A Prayer for Pop
(August 12, 2017)

We pray for our precious Papa Joe
Whose faith in God never wavers or grows low
Swiftly lead him to your light
So he may follow it into the good night.

It's time he's made it home at last—
Let his earthly sufferings fade ultra-fast…
As he leaves the weight of this world behind,
We know his reward will be easy to find.

Thank you, Dad, for shining in His light
For leading us along the path that's right.

May your love live on through those you've shown
That love of light from seeds is grown.

(Resting blissfully with all his dogs, August 13, 2017)

Just So You Know...

Just wanted you to know how much your kindness has meant,
Though I never, ever in my life thought I'd be a "cancer patient"
Sick here I am, yet I just wouldn't be "me"
If I didn't write some kind of poetry

It's easy to see this cancer epidemic is wrong
Once you're exposed, you sing a different life song
Your friendship is what sets me apart from the throng
Your wisdom and strength have been with me all along

If I forget, your sincere words remind me I am strong
Your constant prayers keep my spirit moving along
Some of us have known each other for way too long
Reflecting on our shared memories helps my brain from playing too much ping-pong!!!
With all of you in my corner, it's time to give cancer the final good-bye gong…

So thank you for whatever kindness you've shown me—
It's truly motivating to stay positively cancer FREE!!!

Love,

9-22-16

Dear Friends,

Thank you for your sympathy,
Your kindness and generosity
My father's passing has been surreal to me
Especially
Since my other pop checked out four days later—and years too quickly
I can't describe the sadness that I've been hiding,
And I didn't want to face the school day—no lying!
But seeing all your friendly faces and knowing that you care
Guides me through each day—without you, I'd never dare!

(October 17, 2017)

Birds and Wind Chimes
(For all of us, December 2018)

We go together to visit Dad's the weekend after Christmas,
Squished into the back of my brother's car, safety in numbers
Earlier I chickened out from visiting the grave alone—
An instinctual fear of cemeteries, the dead in general,
And of being anywhere too woodsy by myself—
Dad was dead, after all, but he didn't raise me to be foolish—
Hard not to remember the know-it-all authority in his voice
And his concern, abruptly and sometimes brutally given,
Caring at the heart of him—equally—for anyone deserving

I glanced at the long expanse of Russian Orthodox grave sights
That lay between the car and Dad's area—farthest away of all,
Realized I wasn't sure it was even a proper time to visit,
Thought of my father's common sense and used it to exit
He'd be saying to me, "You'd be a jackass to walk all the way
out here, just before dark, by yourself—dressed like a gypsy—
especially you, LeRoy, tripping around with your hands stuffed in
your pockets. You'll fall right into the grave…"
So I left, feeling some guilt, but a sense of forgiveness also

Another time, my husband and I stopped by to visit "Dad"
And failed to find the grave stone, walking in circles,
Both of us reading the Russian names, feeling stupid,
Searching the tombstones for his easy name: Thomas A. Clark
We must have blocked the location from our memories—
The gloomy burial scene, a relentless cascade of hateful rain
Turning my husband's suit jacket into a pile of lumpy black crepe paper,
Imagining what Dad would be saying about idiots with NYC style
who wear Italian silk to outdoor funerals
We left the cemetery that day, disappointed,
Ashamed of being "North-Jersey-city-slickers, all dressed up,
but too out of touch with the rest of the world to find a grave,"

Until we found out, from my brother and his wife
That the stone hadn't been set up yet, as was the custom

Startled out of my reverie by our arrival at Dad's house,
I follow my brother, his wife, and their son into the yard—
Ghostly memories spook me from behind the white porch furniture
The very last time I saw him alive was out here—
The way we both wanted to remember each other—
Bantering about the birds and the bees with wicker rocking chairs
swinging between us, rather than the truth

Not a trace left of Dad's sickness was visible, but nonetheless,
A tranquility pervading below the senses—his spirit—at peace
No more worries, hushed whispers and tiptoed movements—
Like a broken button, my mind replays the answers to his questions
now that he is gone
We exchange the usual pleasantries, laughter, jokes…
Dad's sense of humor clearly an invisible thread among us
And I remind myself not to look for him anymore…
That I am too sensitive, too sentimental for my own good

I keep it together because my stepmom and sister are so strong
Little Tommy opens presents, and it helps to diffuse the pain
We don't mention his name, the wise white owl in the room
Watching over us in a framed picture with those knowing eyes
That never let on how much his cancer was consuming him
Missing the best years of his life, while his widow moves on,
Still carrying him with her, and with plenty of love leftover
To spend wonderful well-deserved time with great grandbabies
Who will, unfortunately, only know him as a living-room picture

Compelled by sympathy, empathy, I vacate the living room
To have a few, private words with my step-sister
Who would understand that to not speak about it
Wouldn't be my dad's way—we're outspoken people,
Frankly, no need to hide under porch furniture

Being so close, she feels his presence also, as I suspected,
Confirmed by her prayers for his spiritual wellness
Being answered by wind chimes moving without a breeze;
Tiny birds that fly so close, yet are never actually seen,
My dad's spirit would choose to be outside here forever

I never doubted her perception—felt no need to tell her
That I was also visited by a strange, rare bird watching over me
On the morning after she told me the fatal news about Dad.
Nobody else, not even I, would have believed but for sorrow
So I just shook my head in a nod of shared love, grief, and relief.

The Continuity of Grief
(For us—so that we may have our breakfast
moments, at least, January 2019)

Desperately searching for ways to entice my mom to eat,
I pull out one of Pop's cups given to us among his things…
As if it were meant to be there to help me to help her,
As if he knew, even in death, that he would be enamored

She loves his style, funny. His cups are her favorite, go figure.
And a feeling forms in my mind of continuity—
An object bridge between the dead and the living,
As if my wish for them to become good friends has come true,
As if, even if he could return, she would remember who he is

Despite her Alzheimer's forgetfulness, she comments
Every time she sees his cups on my busy kitchen counter,
Among so many other artifacts of those gone before us,
As if my father-in-law planned for it that way, sly fox;
As if he were still a Casanova, the cups are just to her taste

Funny—the way grief will make you hold on to some things,
As if the substitution for a person could be so easily abated,
As if they could still be with us, always and forever

I use Pop's rubber-tipped tongs to flip the breakfast bacon
Thinking of how much he and my husband loved that ritual,
Its spillover into our marriage, its regularity unmatched,
As if in agreement, the tongs catch fire—
As if Pop had his last laugh with us, like old times in the diner

Funny—the way grief will make you hold on to some ideas,
As if you ever had the choice to forget

Full Circle
(January 2019)

Of all the miracles God could have put in my path,
I never would have guessed it would be
Witnessing my mother becoming a child again
For me, it's absolutely incredible,
Having spent my adulthood childless, by choice

Sometimes, she turns back into her fourth-grade self,
Tells me her mother doesn't let her eat French fries
Other times, she becomes her young-adult mother-self,
Wanting to call home to check on her three kids

On her last two-week visit
She looked for her three kids-for us-as I put her to bed
I tucked her in with three monkey beanies instead
And she'll never know I was one of her real monkeys
Peeking in on her from the bedroom doorway,
Making sure she was good and settled and happy…
Coming round
Full circle
Such a comfort to know
She loved us once
And still does
Still our mom,
After all else is lost
Love can still be found

4
Because I Could Not Stop Writing for Death

Josh's Bright Light
In Loving Memory of Joshua Wolf "Clark"
(February 13, 1989–October 9, 2019)

While saying goodbye to my sweet nephew near the ball park
I caught a glimpse of an aura around him like a bright spark;
As I began praying, a voice whispered inside my head saying,
You know this will be the last time you see him…
And too soon our world turned awfully cold and dim.

But then the most powerful voice in my head resounded…
The words in my ears bounded and pounded: The last time without
his Heavenly wings. For Earthly angels leave behind
a trail of light for their loved ones in Nature's brightest things.

Look for it in the stars that shine like fireflies
Even in the darkest black of the coldest night skies.
In ripples of water that splash out from the tide,
On the tippity-top of the sun-kissed mountainside—
That's where Joshua's bright light will always reside!

Find it there amongst the brightest colors of the rainbow,
Shining out from the fullest, most iridescent moon's glow.
Joshua's light lives on to make our world bright
Because He loved us as much as we loved His light!

(Sadly on October 9, 2019)

Never Say Goodbye to Our Boxer Named Monty
(Mont-Mont, Monster, Mister, and C'mon Mont!)

For such a small Boxer, you were a giant at heart,
Your loyalty, bravery, and spirit warmed us right from the start.
You had more nicknames than anyone can recall—
And you came running with love to us for them all!

On our regular neighborhood walk,
People with Boxer Love would stop to talk
Of your handsome face, your muscular stalk;
With Lily by your side, no longer a reason for you to hide and skulk.

The way you wiggle-waggled your stub of a nub made us so proud;
You held it so highly, parading throughout the crowd
That everybody fell in love with you while laughing out loud!
By your Boxer-Love, even our picky Ms. Lily was wowed;
To your Boxer-Heart she remains *furever* vowed!

For a tiny, unwanted rescue, your conformation was second-to-none—
Personality—nothing but unconditional, loveable fun!
We adored hugging your chest, tickling your four white sox—
Forever big in our memories now—resting in peace in your small,
mahogany box.

You cradled us in your paws when we'd lost both our dads to cancer
in the same week;
Now you're gone before I'd realized you'd reached your life's peak!
To my singing, you always wagged your docked, happy tail,
Though my blinded-by-love eyes never saw your lungs beginning to fail.

News of losing you to cancer, a woefully painful surprise—
Since you'd already beaten it once, no way to stifle our shocked cries!
But you told me with your pouty face and those sad Boxer eyes
That those unforeseen lung tumors would cause your ultimate demise.
So we had no choice but to sputter out our desperate goodbyes…

You were sick when we found you, an Angel in Boxer disguise,
You grew to be a miniature mustang with the strongest, most mus-
cular thighs!
That special look held for those you adored reflected deeply in your eyes!
This poem, a reminder and comfort, that Boxer-Love never, ever
truly dies!!

We loved walking you with our pretty, stubborn Lily—
Both of you were so well-behaved and yet so cute and silly;
You were the perfect Mr. and Mrs. like Milly and Vanilly!
Our little Seabiscuit—saved us from such misery clearly;
We loved you so fiercely—and miss you just as dearly!

We trusted your ears to be always on guard—
Losing our little bit of sunshine like this is simply too hard!
Lily's loss shown by saving up His share of chewing bones—
Her own outcry of mourning—a "Mr. Monty Jones!"

You were the perfect Boxer gentleman "fighter"
Watching over me when I needed to be a writer—
And loyally present for each and every "nail-biter"
Somehow you made our many sorrows feel lighter!

Baked tears and chicken in barbeque sauce—
Still crying nonstop, now for my own, personal loss.
Eating store-bought Pub Burgers upside-down
That last night in the kitchen to stop my droopy frown.
You were a world-class table-food beggar and clown!
Another "barbeque chicken-licken hound"
The likes of Monty will never be found!
My eyes filled with tears up to the brim,
A final kiss placed on his lips still outlined in charcoal trim—
Praying he knew how much love we all felt for him!

You once jumped off a tiny fishing dock into a pond—
Of our talented, bravehearted Boxer, we were ever so fond;

The hugs you gave when we needed you most—
When we were sick, it was not the doc, but by you, we were diagnosed!

You'd run through scary tunnels and do anything for a treat;
How you loved playing with every single dog you'd meet—
When I got the cancer, you were forever after found at my feet!
Whenever the toast was on fire, you warned me of danger,
To think that once, to your heart, I was just a stranger!

They said you were four when you came home through our door—
And we guess maybe you died at age eleven—
You were by our sides, every day of every year—almost for seven—
Someday I hope to run around forever with you on the Trails of
Heaven.

My fondest Monty Memory, with all the woodsy, joyful frill—
Is the memory of your spirit running freely, full of pure Monty
Monster thrill—
Rolling boldly in front of us down life's Confidence Hill!

In summer's hot scorch, you darted into Lily's swimming creek—
Even though we all knew your swimming skills were weak—
Horsing around the water at your top Boxer Speed—
A lasting memory of how your spirit was certainly and forever freed!

I never imagined it would be your very last swimming run—
Your leaving us behind on the trail is like taking a shot in the heart
by Life's Misery Gun!
But I knew it was time for you to rise beyond the pain of the cold
earth and the hot sun.

You listened as I wept with grief, humming your favorite Outlander
tune,
Because I needed you to hear my voice before we sent you over the
Earth's moon.

On September 8, 2020, Monty, Beloved Boxer Cosentino, went gently off to sleep…
Running with wings in Doggy Heaven—only Forever in our Hearts to Keep!

"Licken Chicken" in my kitchen, the night before the end of the end—
We love you, Mont-Mont, and can never say goodbye to our best, best friend!

With all my love, devotion, and gratitude;
May God forever enjoy your Boxer Angel Attitude!

Your Mommy,

(January 8, 2021; Revised August 9, 2021)

Lisa Thomas Frey
(1972–2021)

In loving memory of Lisa Thomas Frey,
Steadfast wife and apple of her husband's eye
Wouldn't want us all to stay here and cry why
Instead, she would ask us to face the truth, not deny;
To come to terms with life's too-short lease
And embrace the here and now with love and peace

When the bling from heaven's glow would suit her better
Than simply wearing angel wings on her earthly sweater,
Looking to fill the job of sainthood
And seeing she had checked every box so far as *good*
She would want us to know it was her calling
God's way of filling an empty space to prevent another's falling

Lisa's world was judgement-free; her brain was not on pre-set
She was, indeed, a friend the very first time we met
The word *surrender* was not found in her dictionary
Though sometimes life could seem so altogether scary
Lisa Thomas Frey kept her eye firmly on life's sacred prize
Faithfully loving and caring; despite all odds was most wise

Leaving behind this poem to memorialize her strong belief
She wanted me, through these words, to minimize your grief,
For her tenacity, dignity, loyalty, and grace,
Lisa will forever be a shining star in God's warm embrace!

(Sent with All Her Love from Above, Lisa)
(September 13, 2021)

Hospice Logs
February 2022

They told me in plain old words I curse
That Mom's health had taken a "turn for the worse"
In a panic, I tried hard to accept it—tried hard to explain
That her late-stage, seventy-seven-year-old Alzheimer's brain
Had checked into the COVID-19's Penthouse Suite,
Hanging up the Do Not Disturb for Eternity Sign at her feet

It is up to me now to release her, to bring her *home*
Though my brain is flooding with memories, gratefully I let it roam
As the contrast to my reality settled into my head—
No way to imagine that soon she'd be dead!

Hospice nurse arrives to say she's so strong
But for the brain's going backward and wrong
Sister Morphine will be needed to help her along
No more singing together our favorite theme song!

Like ignorant children, we ride up and down on life's seesaw
As the mercury in our thermometers rises only to fall
Enjoy all of life's music while you can still hear the sound
Before God hits the stop button on your merry-go-round!

When you fight so dearly, so clearly for all you love and know
Consider that the hardest thing about your life will be to let go

Revenge's Sweet Smile
February 21, 2022

Peace for the deceased,
But your grief is increased
For they let go of everything wrong
While you hoe a row of guilt a lifetime long

Guilt stinks worse than any infection—
Reeks with self-loathing retrospection
The power of her own words pre-sealed her fate
Alas, our desperate deeds are coming far too late

Any pain in life I had inflicted, she released at the last
Forgiven as she faded from the reality of my life so fast
Her mercy, but not God's as her earthly body passed

Cold marble spread up to her button-sized, cute nose
Her eyes poised, awaiting the eminence of heaven's doze
While my heart with life's utter wickedness froze

My hand steadied on her heart beating so softly as snow falling and
falling and falling on snow
Whispering my love in her ears as we prayed for her peaceful,
Final "Let Go"

Her DNR sign bravely displayed her No Feeding Tube Code
Because she did not want to be stuck in traffic like her father on
Death's Road

After ten days, her life's spirit decided with a sweet smile to give in…
Why does God deal us a hand, knowing we can never win?

Everlasting   Lasting

Love

Long before birth, a mother's love begins to grow;
Once planted there, with light, it continues to glow

Like a seed inside us that becomes a flower;
It holds us by roots even in our darkest hour

Her love shines on within your heart—
Through memories, never to part—

The love bond formed
upon her labor
remains yours
forever to
savor

The Last Words

Condolence cards
offer words for free
of sadness, comfort, sympathy—
Our loved ones exit
on those final words of empathy;
The painful truth of their death is recognized;
as their favorite "life clips" are kindly summarized

They are spirits now, at peace, in rest, memorialized;
the unfathomable idea of their loss compartmentalized
By expressions that keep their ghosts in the graveyard,
tucked away neatly in a brain file in the mind's drawer—
A familiarly-fond memory in "The Land of Forevermore"

They have gone to let us face our own demons unkind
With well wishes from friends and lovers
they have left behind—
A duty to charge forward
with their loving legacies into time—
Armed with our sunshine daydream memories
And the sentimental words in this rhyme!
(August 1, 2023)

Phoenix in Ash

Phoenix collapsed in a pile of ash, leaving tragically,
My till-death-do-us partner is gone unexpectedly
Caught in mid-flight pattern, a wild bird on fire, declining
Did not see himself flailing, dropping feathers, downward spiraling,
Rather thought himself a rare Phoenix, uniquely death-defying,
Doing pushups and change-ups to keep up with all the lying

To defer my anger, there is only one other I can hurt with the news
Who will know that my better half will not be paying her dues;
The model he gave our secrets and money to "online"
That his fake, dirty voice is stilled, lusty hazel eyes no longer shine

Forgiveness graces him as life's victim, not "Just an Addict"
His power over me fueled his hellfire, doctored his sex script
I looked for extra jobs to pay for *our* alternative lifestyle—
He hid the needle tracks under his bright plumage the whole while

Living in shadow can make you seek the comforts of a dark night;
I would rather face the pain in the day's truthful bright light
Had he confided in me, we could have won that Last Good Fight,
Springing up from the ashes of his past to take forward flight

Senselessly, I plot revenge on that porn slut and her industry
For wrecking real love under the guise of sex, freedom, and liberty
But can picture her dumb-struck and wrapped up in cheap lingerie
To her, Phoenix was another plain, old thousand-dollar day
She was still pocketing the filthy fee, while he fought not to OD.
I lost my hand-fast, best friend when he became his worst enemy

Alone in my own peace; the Guilty-Self-War must come to cease!

No shadows bear nor block the growth of love's labor's frost
Survival code mandates that your lover is and forever will be lost.
"Letting go" of ashes, a love spark burst; gloomy shadow flew
My spirit, then, with blazing warm faith suddenly did renew

Anger masks the pain that cannot be shirked—leaves us walking lame,
From "the life" we knew, the real one, and the one that never came
Could Phoenix have risen upon another given chance?
Or would he have fallen in the same ashen circumstance?

My Phoenix had it all, yet traded his life for a lethal dose of Fentanyl.

Leanne Cosentino
(December 1, 2023; Revised March 21, 2024)

5
Jersey Shorts Stories

Twists and Turns

If I had to pick one important thing to share that I have learned from experience, it would be to not build up expectations by overplanning. Sometimes life can take you down unexpected roads, despite all your mapping. Such was the case in how I found my husband.

I had been, and I am not embarrassed to admit it, in search of a husband ever since turning thirty. Although I am not a traditionalist, I somehow felt my marriage clock ticking. If you are familiar with the Jersey Shore area, you know it can be quite difficult to find a decent guy who is more interested in you than in how his biceps look in a T-shirt. In my search, I had encountered several failed relationships, as well as disappointingly strange blind dates. Eventually, I resolved to give myself a break and decided to date my hairstylist instead. He was a good-looking, well-groomed, and funny guy who was straight, believe it or not. Right away I had him pegged as a *player* and made sure he knew that I knew it.

The problem was that he was ten years younger, so I approached our relationship very casually, even though what I wanted really was a husband. I even told him the way I felt. I think it went something like this: "This relationship is great because I can date you and still look for a husband at the same time." Ironically, it was my casual attitude that finally attracted him to me…and he proposed, to my astonishment! Imagine finding love at the Jersey Shore! More importantly, if I had expected him to propose, I would have behaved differently and ultimately been disappointed when my plans failed.

The way he proposed to me also threw a twist into my journey down Expectation Road. You see, I am a planner, and he is extremely spontaneous. In fact, he lacks a filter for his thoughts to sift through before they pour out of his mouth. Ironically, I appreciate this in him, as I don't have to worry that he might lie to me—he tells me everything, whether he intends to or not! So one beautiful, crisp November day, he invited me to the city to look at diamond rings. He swore it was for fun, you know, in case he wanted to propose. Hypothetically, he would have a better idea of what to get me.

Did I mention he was impulsive? His proposal could best be described using the same adjective. Within one hour, he had picked out, purchased, and shown me the ring, saying, "We make a good team. Will you marry me? I don't want to wait [big surprise] because I know I want to spend the rest of my life with you." The lights in the store were flickering a closing-time warning, so there was no time for any sort of romance such as a bent-knee or surprise announcement (yeah, right!). Did I have time to respond before the store closed? You better believe I accepted his offer ASAP before he changed his mind, closing time or not!

What were my expectations for a solid relationship? Well, to be truthful, romance was at the top of my list until I realized my husband was very far from romantic. For example, on my last birthday, I told him all I wanted was "a little romance," maybe just dinner for two and a local comedy show. Instead, he invited one of his clients (an older "aunty-type") to dinner with us. He never told her it was my birthday because he knew she would try to pick up the bill and did not want to do that to her. Sweet of him? Well, certainly it was not romantic! Did I get upset? A hundred years ago, I probably would have, but I have grown to appreciate my real relationship, not my expectations for it.

My experiences with the twists and turns in life's journey have taught me to understand that you cannot have too many expectations, not even for your spouse. As if to prove it to myself, later that night, I opened a package I received earlier in the mail from a close, sentimental college friend. She lives in Florida but never fails to send me a birthday gift. Although I usually do not wear it, I was pleasantly surprised to see a little bottle of perfume. You will never guess the name of the perfume she sent. Of course, it was called Romance!

So you see, you usually get just what you need from life—if not from your husband, then from a true friend. Appreciate the reality of your relationships and cherish the unexpected twists and turns that show up in your life's road!

Little Things Are Big

When I was just a little girl, I used to get excited about the approaching holidays. My mother did not always share my enthusiasm, but my father did. He was always ready to make me feel special on holidays. How did he accomplish this feat? He would get me something little but perfect to celebrate.

My favorite was a heart-shaped box of chocolates on Valentine's Day. It was a little thing, but it was very big for me. I came to expect a teddy bear and chocolates, as well as a special card every Valentine's Day. As I got older, of course, my dad stopped getting me Valentines, but the little girl in me still and always will long for a heart-shaped box of chocolates!

It doesn't matter what the little thing is. What is important is that your loved one made the effort to do something to make you feel just a little bit happier! Little things like that can make a huge difference in someone's day because feeling loved is always BIG.

Recently, my husband, who is like my mother regarding holidays, heard a little statistic about people driving to work. A study revealed that if a couple kissed each other goodbye before leaving for work, the couple would have a 50 percent less chance of getting into an accident on the road.

Usually, my husband does not make a BIG deal about saying goodbye…so I was surprised to see him running out the door to give me a kiss goodbye (he thought he had forgotten to in the house). As he did, he laughed and said, "Fifty percent chance less!" As I drove off smiling, I couldn't stop thinking about how BIG the little things can be—and it wasn't even close to being Valentine's Day!

May the little things always be BIG for you too!

(June 15, 2016)

Lost and Found Family Baggage

A while ago, when airport security was just beginning to get beefed up, my brother and I arrived at the Philadelphia Airport for our trip to Florida. Prior to leaving, I had packed up my suitcase and a bag for him as well, as he had to work late and was afraid we would miss the flight, otherwise.

It was chilly in New Jersey, and because I had left straight from work, there were books, a coat, a pocketbook, teacher bags, dirty clothes, and other unnecessary items that I wouldn't need. I packed up my belongings that I didn't want to take to Florida with me, and I set them aside in a big black bag that I found at my mother's house. There was a smaller, traveling bag on wheels I packed for myself and another black, striped bag that had a nice handle-strap for my brother's belongings. It was just going to be the two of us on the trip. I had recently become engaged, and somehow our schedules matched up enough to celebrate with this vacation. Usually, my brother and I get along well, and like my father, he's such a great planner that I didn't worry about anything when traveling with him!

My brother gets very nervous, though, and I wasn't surprised when he inquired about my bag. "You didn't pack anything stupid, like scissors, did you? You know there are so many new regulations since 911, and I don't want any delays. We're running late enough already." Surely enough, I had packed a pair of cuticle scissors in my makeup clutch, so I rummaged through the small bag and recovered the questionable item, placing it in the big black bag I intended to keep in the back of the SUV.

Of course, being a male, my brother paid little attention to my description of the black striped bag he was supposed to grab and picked up the big black bag instead. Of course, I trusted he would recognize the black striped bag since it came out of his closet and never noticed he was carrying the wrong bag into the airport.

You can imagine the panicked look on his face at the X-ray baggage line, as the attendants approached him, and carried off his bag. The scissors had, indeed, set off an alarm; the problem, of course, was that the items were unrecognizable to my brother because they were mine.

Tom thought the woman behind him must have mixed up the bags, and he told the attendants as much. I was safely through already and waiting anxiously especially because I couldn't see what was happening. Occasionally I saw Tom's face, and it was not looking good. What could have happened? He tried to mouth the words to me through the glass, but I am an especially poor lip reader, and nearly blind with nearsightedness, so it was useless. Finally, I saw the big black bag in question, but I did not recognize it either, as it was not the black, striped bag that I had packed for him.

Suddenly, I saw attendants pulling out the contents, as my brother swore and swore it wasn't his bag—he was becoming hysterical now, thinking his own bag was stolen, and what this would mean for our trip. He tried everything possible not to be late, and this unforeseen drama was very unlikely, unexpected, and beyond his level of self-control.

It took some time for me to figure out the contents of the bag were mine, as I was so far away, literally and figuratively—I had no clue that the bag contained my "undesirables," even after I watched the security crew pull out books, teacher bags, my own pocketbook… wait…my panties (eeek) and then it was too late. They found my teacher's ID card and announced the name of the bag's owner so that they could switch the bags back as my brother suggested. Imagine the shocked look on my face when they paged me! Of course, I was mortified to have to admit that the bag was mine. How could this mix-up ever be explained? I told them the silly story, using as few words as possible to lessen the shocked look on their faces, and on my brother's puzzled face. Somehow they believed us, maybe because it was just too stupid to not be the truth, and we were siblings, after all. Obviously, idiocy ran in our family.

They allowed Tom to return the bag and switch it for the black striped bag with the great handle, and as he left, it would be impossible to forget the look on his face as his eyes met mine. This time I understood clearly his mouthed words as they matched my own. "Idiot!"

"You should have left that big black bag at home!"

"You should have paid attention or packed your own bag!"

Fortunately, we had enough time to successfully proceed through the safety zones, grab a bite to eat, and enjoy a well-needed Margarita before boarding time. The trip was typical, and we enjoyed our time, for the most part, until we found some trouble in paradise. We decided to hit all the theme parks and be very active during the day, saving the last night to go out to bars and have some party time.

With all the hustle and bustle at the baggage area, the security workers had failed to check my brother's license properly. We found out when the attendants refused to let my brother wear the drinking bracelet at Disney's Paradise Island. You can only wear the bracelet if you're over twenty-one. Though Tom was thirty-six at the time, his license had expired, unbeknown to him, me, and The Philadelphia International Airport.

Although I offered to sneak him the drinks, he declined; I mean, his license showed his age, after all. He just wanted to leave and sit at a boring piano bar. Back then, I was young at heart and wanted to go dancing and partying, but that idiot couldn't even make sure he had a valid license to party! We fought like only brothers and sisters can in front of the huge crowd of people entering Paradise Island. I don't remember most of the words we used, but I do recall that he told me I should make sure to marry my fiancé immediately because he couldn't understand how anyone would want to do that, and I should jump on the opportunity before he changed his mind. I think I snorted out something about his being such a boring sissy that he was too afraid to drink a beer without the bracelet!

Eventually we came to terms and spent time at both venues, enjoying the last night of this vacation that we had thought lost. We needed to think about how he would return to Jersey with an expired license. After some discussion, we concluded that the airline workers were to blame for this—of course, he wouldn't have been allowed to fly at all with the expired license, but that didn't matter to us…we had enjoyed some beers by now and apologized mostly for the nasty things we'd said to each other, finding our sibling bonds renewed. As we reviewed our returning flight information, thinking about the airport, we simultaneously looked up and said "IDIOTS!"

Live a Little

Doctors are such smart people—I always value their opinions, whether I agree or not with what they're saying, but it's the approach that matters. The personal touch is what differentiates the good from the bad doctor, but the approach is what makes me make that second appointment. Doctors, like teachers, can take the high or the low road I guess when communicating with their patients or students. You can be the sage on the stage and just come out with it, jargon and all, or be less direct in your guidance, the guide by the side. I prefer both methods and will settle for a little of both in healthcare or other professionals—my doctors all are very human, and mostly that's why I like them because I don't usually focus on my physical health now that I'm so sad with my mom. Any healthcare visit sends me into PTS disorder from cancer—I don't think about it beforehand or anything, but a quick, routine visit to the gynecologist now sends me bursting into tears (on the table, of course) for no apparent reason.

Today's visit was different because Dr. G gave her sage advice about Mom and made me feel normal about the whole thing. It was free mental health with my routine examination! Thanks for that, Doc. She was dead-on-and with wisdom from experience—lots of concern for my family as well. Go figure. So I cried with good reason as we talked about what was to come next in this dying game. She bluntly, yet compassionately, told me that it's only a matter of time before she has physical ailments too serious for any of us to handle, and so pray for letting go and for her comfort. She agreed that it's possible for me to still enjoy her company and vice versa as long as she continues to have her memory moments. Allowing me to continue this mind map of the near future helps to say goodbye a little every time-she suggested. What a sage-on-the-stage approach! Glad she hit me over the head with that dose of reality I needed. She is my mom, and I will know when I can no longer handle her. Maybe? She assured me that it was normal to think of how she's dying a little every day, but so are the rest of us, and it's just a fact.

It was not easily done, but it felt good to get that bit of confidence. My other doctor takes the low-road approach. It took me days to figure out what he meant when he told me the story about his mom with Alzheimer's in the home. His aunt came and fed her the chocolate-covered raisins they both loved, and it brought such a smile to her face, and to his in recollection, but I had no clue what he was trying to tell me. It hit me one night as Mom and I enjoyed some sun outside in the spring air, commenting on birds and trees like we South Jersey Girls do. I realized my doctor was a genius. I don't need to do much to enjoy Mom's company because we're so sim-ple—it's the simple, easy things—enjoying your time that matters, not what you do! What a relief! To think I was laughing at my doc's silliness and the whole time he made me learn something invaluable! Experiencing simple laughter and enjoyment is the stuff that sticks in memories.

With this perspective in mind, slowing down for the first time in my adult life, I enjoyed spring and was very glad Mom was here with me. She may not remember it, but I will. My backyard bird sanctuary was just what we needed to bond—wild, free-spirited, and peaceful like my mom. Remember to live a little each day while dying along the way!

Missing the Boat
September 18, 2023 (Revised March 20, 2024)

Once upon a sunny time, I married you, gladly. My trepidations were only for your flightiness—but I knew your love was steady as we rocked the boat together on Society's Jersey Shore. At first, the ten-year age difference, my being "a cougar" to boot, caused mild waves that made it seem like it would always be just you and me. You and I, in marital love on our own tiny fantasy island surrounded by naysaying waters we ignored with impunity. We swam together back then by the gently stirring waters near the sandbar until cloudy weather created such a misty fog that we drifted off course. Stormy tidal waves soon followed, one after another, and then another—so many that pulled us down, right in front of my tear-strained, tidal-waved eyes that I missed our boat as it sailed away to brighter shores, leaving us both stranded on Fantasy-Free Island. You followed the Cocaine Waterway for a long ride until smacking into a rip tide, while I was wrapped up in hemp rope trying to stay by your side.

So alone on our own Misery Moat, minus the Love Boat, we treaded water, apart. You never tried to find me either, hiding behind your iPad goggles, viewing mermaids, but not seeing me as I was still trying to do laps on our rocky shore. There were a few times, after we spotted a rainbow or had an unexpectedly good old beach party, that we viewed each other with some hopes of wading in the baby section once more, holding hands and jumping foamy, gentle waves with ease. Somehow those waves rippled by and were lost to us. I wanted a sea captain, but you wanted me to act like a mermaid!

You were supposed to navigate with me through the rest of our days in that Love Boat. Instead, shipwrecked, I'm moving your clothes to forget, like the rest of this mess, just for now—just some shelter from the thoughts I can't see yet—shelter—from the visions of that night—my bobby pin entrance after trying seven other tools to makeshift the skeleton key to enter the locked purple bathroom, not even knowing yet that you were in any danger until I couldn't hear the snoring, no gurgling, no drowning sounds, then no sounds at all except my heart pounding to action to be your hero and extending the life-vest way too late!

It took me a few salt-rimmed drinks to move your coats so that I do not have to see them and cry every time I get the vacuum or need a shopping bag. I loved your outerwear—every hat, scarf, glove, and hoodie is in great taste. Our twenty years of marriage, too, was such a good-looking shameful waste. I search through each coat pocket every time I open the closet into that realm—feeling as lost a soul as the traitor, Brother Edmund in Narnia, except with a purple-clad Queen Fentanyl playing the role of The White Witch, offering you heroin instead of yum-yums; her long arm constricting your throat and ending with needle fingers. You were always so taken in by both the color purple and sweets, that I am not surprised. I am lost in the coats in my closet looking for clues. I search for the theme of this tragedy, for anything that might explain what I did wrong—or what mistake you may have made by accident, but I find nothing, not even a pack of matches, nor a warm, glowing lamppost to guide me out of this frozenness. I am lost in the cold in the coat closet. I find nothing, nothing but cold nothingness.

Everything I saved is in the closet in your man cave room. I have emptied out your dresser—the importance of keeping it so neat overwhelms me now—and it seems the saddest of all the ironic truths to date: that you shaved, bathed, sorted, organized, cleaned, and fixed up everything but yourself that week. Instead of laundry, I had to pick you up off the bathroom floor and try to sort you out, revive you—my partner—my best friend, my husband, and boat-rocking partner!

Thinking of Romeo and Juliet and knowing a lonely life was better than no life, I wiped the foamy white remains of poison off your lips and gave you mouth-to-mouth, our last earthly kiss. The 911 paramedics told me to do chest compressions, as seen only on TV, but in real life, I was not getting through to your cold, purple-stone carcass. You were lying in a puddle of shower water under the Jaws shower curtain, his mouth open for business. You smiled at us, a weak, side-swiping grin, and your eyes rolled back as if to say, "Hey, guys, better late than never, and thanks, but no thanks."

The local paramedics arrived and I watched and prayed out loud as they administered five rounds of Naloxone, shocking your already-done-quit-this-scene-body but not overcoming the poisonous coma inflicted by The Purple Witch. I did not know what you had done to yourself this time, so I showed them the two folds I had found in the garbage pail, still in denial that it could be self-inflicted. Nobody could find a spoon or a needle floating nearby the scene.

They continued with oxygen, and I don't even know what else because having already missed the boat, I desperately staggered to the safety of craggy old sea rocks a while ago, in an effort of last-minute, mid-life self-preservation. That must be why I let them pick you up like a wet old sock and drag you out with the dirty Overdose Loads, not my boat-rocking, white-washed sea captain anymore. They never gave up on you—the paramedics who raced here to save you from yourself—from your circling, shark-toothed, wide-mouthed demons—but we were too late for heroics—and you left me waiting alone in the middle of the beginning of the rest of our lives to watch Outlander Season Seven, Episode Three, titled: "Death Be Not Proud." You know it was weeks before I could watch it, and even then, I doubled up my meds prior, and was not convinced that you had not planned it like this, given your timing, the title, and that you had asked me to watch it with you the night of your date, also, with The Fentanyl Queen.

They took you to the hospital in an ambulance to continue their work on your body and let me see you after they had finally given up after four hours. I was wearing painting clothes because I was staining wood in the yard earlier and never had the chance to get changed. You said I looked cute, to my surprise, when you were my husband and not a corpse I had to face. Your eyes were closed this time, and I had to open one just to make sure you were not still here, realizing that there would be no fix this time. I fit my hand inside of yours to not forget how nice it felt, wondered why I never tried to do that more often, and knew how incredibly much I had lost in that single moment. I don't know what happened next, honestly, because grief will cause you to do some silly things that even I have blocked from memory.

They left the breathing apparatus attached to your face, so I kissed your forehead and thought that it could still be you, sleeping in your apnea mask, but you would be snoring loudly, or asking about breakfast and yelling at the news channel by now. Next, I shot a picture of you with my cell phone, as if I were about to enter it into a "Just Say No to Drugs" poster contest. I professed my love and faithfulness and forgave you with a quickness that even surprised me. In case you were not paying attention like usual, I told you to go to the light, though I knew you would have already done so without hesitation except for your attention deficit disorder. At such a loss, and without you, the bad times expert, to tell me what to do, I pretended I was Claire Fraser, brave surgeon and time traveler from Outlander, saying goodbye to her dead first husband.

Letting pragmatics take over, at least in pretense, I departed, telling myself it was not the first time I had to leave you looking dead in a hospital bed, but sure that it was the very last time. I carried the plastic, draw-string bag containing your soggy, cut-up wet pants—a plaid blue Tommy Bahama pajama, and let my neighbor take me away because I was in shock on the inside, but acting like someone else on the outside. Years of having to "fake it" and maintain composure in front of students, teachers, parents, and administrators made me a better actress than I could have imagined myself. I was thanking the sympathetic hospital staff. Though I could not visit that dark place in public yet, some of the staff were crying for my dead husband who was both young and handsome still, even in death.

The birds were chirping their daily prayers when my neighbor left me at home to try to get some sleep. I had nodded off a bit in bed and awoke in an instant hearing your voice calling me to the laundry basket to check your pants' right-side pocket. The needle was there, toothy and sharp, but tucked away tightly. The syringe was visibly emptied, its contents, along with my last weak drop of hope, washing away in the powerful tides at sea.

You were pronounced gone at 1:46 a.m., but I knew it already when I could no longer see our boat—knew I'd lost you long ago straggling in those waves while I stumbled onto the shore—working on us nevermore.

Instead, I see your clothes when I want to remember the love we never got to restore; searching for the goodbye note I thought you buried in a shirt pocket or sock drawer. Smelling your hats that have yet to be washed, I wonder as I wail, moving like a snail, how I will ever be able to let the rest of you go—my house all full of your stylish, good-looking stuff and comfortable-as-forever antiques that were your father's and my mother's father's, ours, mine. Limping out of tide pools, somehow I have already begun, drawn by the healing call of the warm, drying sun.

Eulobituary for Mr. Dante Gerard Cosentino
(May 16, 1978–July 1, 2023)

As a child, he rode dirt bikes and played football in a league and liked to start fires in the backyard! He was not only the best-dressed, best-looking prom king but also the fastest short-distance track runner in high school. He was athletic and loved boxing, fighting, and playing football when he was younger.

As an adult, he loved watching college and professional football. He was a fan of the NY Giants—whether they had a good or bad season. His attitude was reflective of his philosophy—he was a defender of the underdog and had a huge heart for those less fortunate. Dante was passionate about his causes and voiced his opinions without reservation. Maybe because he never forgot how his big brother defended him at great cost in high school, he would stick his neck out to defend those being bullied. In our neighborhood, he was known to be a loving caretaker to my mother, personally overseeing and nursing her during her final days on hospice with us. He was also known to be a self-appointed vigilante against robbery and drunk driving. He single-handedly stopped two drivers, at separate times, who had caused serious property damage to our neighbors.

Dante was well known for his love of dogs and rode his bike and frequented off-leash dog parks with all of ours, starting conversations with strangers along the route, especially if they had dogs, interesting hair, or were in the military. He loved food more than anything in the world and was the best customer in all the restaurants, delis, pizza places, and convenience stores around us. He was fond of going to Wendy's to spoil our dog Lily who sat shotgun! Rita's was his favorite place to frequent. He was always the very first person waiting, unabashedly, in the line for them to open on the first day of spring! He loved joking and laughing with anyone who seemed likeminded and was my personal sounding board for all my stories, poems, jokes, dreams, obsessions, and dilemmas.

Recently, he joined an Aveda Salon in Shrewsbury and was excited to begin creating his portfolio to build a new clientele and showcase his "old school" cutting techniques. He was hoping to be able to hone his skills with the Aveda products as well—in honor of his father. Dante was a highly artistic and talented hairstylist who had a devoted following of clients who enjoyed his company and conversation as much as their stylish hairdos. He had a way of magnetizing his friends with his charisma, drawing people into his thoughts, causes, and dramas! When you sat in his chair to get your hair done, you felt so at home in his hands!

He was just as talented at getting into trouble as he was at doing hair, but his truer passion was for riding horses. He loved Western-style and dressage—making his horse dance and bow, and riding fast and free in the backwoods. When he could, Dante enjoyed freshwater fishing and was interested in sports, debating, antiques, politics, finances, art, coins, fashion, cinema, weight training, dogs, cards, slot cars, motorcycles, trips to New Hope, and the couch.

Dante was a fan of science fiction series like The Hunger Games and Stranger Things. He especially loved anything related to the 80s and would play Eighties Love Songs Station on Pandora when he drove me to my chemotherapy sessions, miraculously never missing a single appointment! He became hooked on the Outlander series, thanked me for having introduced him to it, and couldn't watch another historical fiction movie or series without trashing it because he was that loyal to our show!

Dante was a loyally fierce friend, especially during the worst times. There were things I could say to him that I would not dream of saying to another person, and he had this special way of putting things in perspective, very bluntly, but assuredly. It was during the most difficult and depressing times in my life that I could count on him to say, "Ah, what are you going to do?" He had a way of knowing what to do when things were not going well and when you least expected it! Donkey was the very first person to come to mind if ever you were in trouble, were treated unfairly, or just needed someone to help fuel your fire if you lacked the energy!

Often, clients and friends would ask me how I "put up with Dante's behavior." Because it was not easy to have a best friend who was his own worst enemy, I would think of a quote from the movie Dirty Dancing, "When you love someone, you love everything about them." Over the past twenty-three years, we had our share of fights, arguments, debates, and debacles, but throughout we shared a sense of humor that allowed us to laugh together through the worst of times; and for that, I will be forever grateful for my best friend, to uphold a sense of playful joy, daily, in his memory. Because even if you didn't always like what he was doing, Dante was impossible not to love! Being loved by Dante was like finding a warm, bright fire while lost in the middle of the coldest, darkest tunnel. If you were that lucky to get close enough to him while heading down his one-way lane, you would be drawn in by the warmth easily, forsaking all others in your belief that marriage means teamwork and is full of examples of "for better or for worse" and "in sickness and in health." I wonder why we have yet to include mental health in that oath!

My brother jokingly referred to Dante as "The Inferno," and perhaps you had a glimpse or two of such a fiery temper. I understood that underneath such anger lurked a painful sadness he would do anything to try to avoid. Unfortunately, anger and numbness do not create the set of coping tools required to live during such circumstances as we endure in today's world. Dante was fiercely independent in spirit, but believed faithfully in God, if not religion itself. He thought he was strong and wise enough to cure himself, but failed despite any interventions, institutions, discussions, and medications. Although he had the best intentions, people skills, and fighting spirit, he was finally outsmarted by a foe he tried but could not beat—himself!

I wish that I could tell you I have made sense out of this tragedy or stopped asking myself that impossible question—why? I have learned that grief is not a process involving time or attitude but a cyclic journey uniquely individual, hopefully leading to a form of acceptance of God's plan, and so I imagine him at peace.

Dante was truly a one-of-a-kind, special, and unforgettable artist! He epitomized the saying, "Beauty is in the eye of the beholder." He lived to create and appreciate beauty in all its forms! His loss will be bitterly felt by all of us who loved him dearly. May he be lovingly remembered resting in the most blissful peace with dogs, telling silly jokes with his handsome grin, eating pizza and ice cream galore, smoking Newports guiltlessly, pumping iron painlessly, creating angelic hairdos colorfully, while surrounded by the fastest, toughest, most beautiful free-spirited wild horses in God's Pasture.

To My Precious, Dante…Resting in peace, forever loved!

ABOUT THE AUTHOR

Leanne Cosentino from Brick, New Jersey, is a reading specialist who worked in public education for over thirty years as a high-school English teacher, adult literacy educator, and elementary and middle-school reading specialist. She achieved a supervisor's certification from Farleigh Dickinson University, a master of reading specialist degree from Kean University, and English and elementary teaching credentials from Rowan University. She graduated summa cum laude from both Rowan and Kean. Leanne has worked with both adults and children in various settings, including adjunct graduate courses, parent workshops, and elementary classroom modeling and support.

Winning the Teacher of the Year Award in her district in two different schools, Leanne was well-received by teachers and students for her work in promoting best literacy practices through in-class modeling, intervention pull-out, and intervention and referral services support. Leanne is very passionate about teaching all learners to grow into lifelong literacy lovers. By simultaneously writing for her career and her personal life, she has persevered through some of life's toughest times.

A resident of the Jersey Shore, she enjoys collecting shells, rocks, and antiques; writing poetry, creating readers' theater scripts and dramatic responses to literature; painting landscapes, playing piano, and reading fantasy and historical fictional novels in a series. Her favorite times are spent outside soaking up the sights and sounds of nature with her beloved dogs. It was outside on a fresh, bright day, at age four, that Leanne created her first poem about spring. Too young to write the words, she dictated it to her mom to write for her. To this day, she believes in the restorative, therapeutic value of writing in any form and the need to share and develop the gift of writing in others. This collection of "shorts" is a creative memoir and an absolute must-read for adults struggling with life's realities—love, health, institutions, addiction, dementia, and death.